❀ A
HEDGE
OF
ROSES ❀

A Hedge of Roses

Jewish Insights into Marriage and Married Life

❀

by

NORMAN LAMM

PHILIPP FELDHEIM, INC.

New York

FELDHEIM PUBLISHERS
200 Airport Executive Park
Spring Valley, NY 10977

Printed in Israel

"Thy body is a heap of wheat, hedged with roses."

— SONG OF SONGS 7:3

"A man marries a woman. She says to him: I have seen what looks like a red rose; and he separates from her. What kind of wall is there between them? What sort of serpent has stung him? What is it that restrains him? — the words of the Torah!"

— MIDRASH PSALMS 2:15

Preface to the Fifth Edition

In the eight years since *A Hedge of Roses* first appeared it has been reprinted a number of times, in several languages. I confess that I am pleasantly surprised by the gratifying acceptance it has been accorded.

During this time, I have received a number of suggestions and criticism by colleagues, students, reviewers, and other readers. Many of their recommended changes are incorporated in this edition, even as others have been included in the periodic revisions since the first edition. I have, furthermore, modified a number of expressions or allusions which were more appropriate to the 60's than the 70's. However, the structure, even the text itself, remain basically unchanged, save for Chapter VI, which contains a summary of

Family Purity, and which first appeared in the fourth edition, printed in 1972.

One of the major changes that have occurred since *A Hedge of Roses* was first published, is the emergence of a concentrated attack on marriage itself. A number of novelists, psychologists, Women's Lib advocates, and others have subjected marriage to scathing criticism and found it wanting.

It is difficult to tell whether it is the failure of so many marriages that has brought the institution of marriage itself into disrepute, or whether it is the other way around. Probably both premises are true. On the one hand, the experience of wrecked and miserable marriages inspires advocacy of a "life-style" in which individuals find "self-realization" without the restraints and tensions of marriage. On the other hand, the "swinging" philosophy of a sexually active celibacy further erodes strained marital relationships by holding up a seductive model of a hedonist's paradise: sex without marriage, fun without fanfare, privilege without responsibility — and all respectable, of course.

Our purpose here is not to plead the cause of marriage, which will survive in any case. The modish "cop-out" simply disguises disinclination as principle; personal cowardice is more acceptable if presented as social criticism. Our intention, rather, is to address those who have decided to risk marriage — both its pains and pleasures, its restraints and its opportunities. It is to such people that these pages are directed, in the hope that an awareness of the dangers to marriage will underscore the personal growth and fulfillment that may be found in and because of it, and that this in turn will lead young people to

listen attentively to what the Jewish tradition has to say about a special method of
enhancing the relationship they are contemplating.

Norman Lamm

Lake Como, Penna.
June 26, 1974.

TABLE OF CONTENTS

Author's Foreword

This work is an attempt to present, in a manner meaningful to the modern Jew and Jewess, a Jewish institution that is as sacred as it is ancient, as precious as it is unknown, and as vital as it is misunderstood.

Hopefully, this tract will contribute in some small measure both to the preservation of a Jewish precept that ranks amongst the noblest in all of Judaism, and to the stability and happiness of the Jewish home.

Most marriages are failures. That simple, stark, devastating fact must be impressed upon every young couple contemplating marriage. If the purpose of marriage is to unite two people in love, to bestow upon them a feeling of fulfillment and the glow of serenity, then the majority of marriages simply fail to achieve their purpose. Whether or not they end in divorce, all too many marriages become exercises in sustained tension, only occasionally relieved by periods of happiness and joy. To ignore this, and to undertake the responsibilities of married life under the dangerous romantic illusion that happiness is inevitable "because we love each other," is to invite misery and frustration.

Marriage is one of the most far-reaching decisions any human being is called upon to make in the course of a life-time. The consequences are too staggering, too momentous, to tolerate casualness and thoughtlessness. The odds, in our tense and changing society, are heavily weighted against a tolerable, let alone a happy marriage. Yet all too often young people enter into marriage with no more foresight than they give to the choice of a school or to the selection of a new dress. Even when the choice of a partner for life is exercised with intelligence and maturity, there is an unspoken assumption that all will go well without further attention because, after all, "love conquers all." This is dangerous nonsense, and results in the focusing of all creative energies and concerns on the trivial details of the *wedding* while blissfully ignoring the larger questions of the *marriage*.

Such an attitude is the prelude to domestic disaster. With all honor to romantic love, it simply is incapable of solving all problems, even all marital problems. At best, marriage between two people, who are usually young, of limited experience, and who have known each other but briefly, is a risky venture. The disruptive forces of our times, the violent changes that have transformed our society and wrenched it loose from its secure moorings and made impermanence and uncertainty the distinctive landmarks of our lives, have played havoc with marriage — which, ultimately, is based upon trust and permanence, upon certainty and continuity. The prospects are dim for true bliss for any couple — unless there is a conscious effort by young people on the threshold of marriage to seek out in advance whatever insurance they can to strengthen the home they are about to build.

The discipline known as Family Purity, to which these pages are dedicated, will at first appear strange to those who have never heard of it. It is not an easy one, in the beginning. Even those raised in an observant Jewish home will at first find these restraints difficult. But, while there can be no absolute guarantees, there is nothing that can quite equal the effectiveness of this institution in reinforcing the fiber of domestic life. Any young person of intelligence and sensitivity, vitally concerned with making his or her marriage

14

work, will find the discipline of Family Purity positively delightful and, ultimately, indispensable.

The Jewish family, traditionally, may not have been overly demonstrative in expressing affection outwardly. Yet love was everpresent, the bedrock of the home, as solid and reliable as the ancient and sacred tradition from which the character of our people is hewn. Squeamishness never allowed the sexual nature of this marital love to be overlooked or minimized; modesty never permitted it to be vulgarized and dishonored. And the "hedge of roses," the periodic restraints of Family Purity, purified it, exalted it, and ennobled it.

The reader must not assume that the subject is treated comprehensively in these pages. This is no more than an introduction to the theme; in fact, it is totally inadequate for the actual practice of Family Purity, for which certain manuals are available and which will be recommended by name later.

No claim to originality is made for the ideas herein presented. Some of them were heard by the author, directly and indirectly, from a number of his distinguished teachers and learned colleagues in the rabbinate and on the various faculties of Yeshiva University. Whatever merit may pertain to this work, the author happily shares with them; the shortcomings are his alone.

Most of this essay was originally presented as a lecture to the Young Married's Club of The Jewish Center, whose cordial and approving reception was most encouraging. Mr. Philipp Feldheim, publisher, deserves special commendation for urging the author to commit it to writing and for volunteering to print it as a public service.

Norman Lamm

Lake Como, Penna.
July 28, 1965

Sexuality and Morality

The laws of Family Purity are a marvelous educational device. They teach us Judaism's insights into the nature of sex and, by extension, certain truths about human personality. These insights are of perennial relevance, today no less than ever before.

The Ancient-Modern Dilemma

The exciting psychological (especially psychoanalytic) theories developed in the earlier decades of this century by Freud and his school, the well-documented statistical studies of sexual behaviour of Americans by

Prof. Kinsey and his successors, and the much heralded "sexual revolution" of the present decade, have complicated rather than simplified contemporary man's personal view of sex. Our problems have been deepened, not solved. Those benighted souls who have opted to "be modern" and "play it cool" by abandoning the restraints imposed by traditional moral standards have deluded themselves into thinking that they have espoused a new "philosophy of sex" when, in fact, they have dared nothing more than plain, old-fashioned libertinism out of a sense of exasperation and despair.

Indeed, for all our sophistication and smart terminology, we moderns are confronted, essentially, by two contradictory concepts of sexual conduct, each of which is fundamentally a restatement of an ancient attitude towards sex. And, paradoxically, most of us in fact embrace both views — and

18

suffer endlessly from the resulting inner contradictions.

On the conscious level, we assimilate all the openness towards sex of our post-Freudian society. There are, apparently, no secrets left any longer. Enlightened, knowing all the answers from our very earliest youth, we are also "emancipated": we strip sex of its shroud of mystery, which we consider mere romantic nonsense, look upon it as nothing more than a natural biological urge, and condemn traditional religious and moral standards as hypocritical at worst and guilt-breeding and neurosis-inducing prudery at best. *Playboy* is the Bible of our "sexual revolution"; its various imitators and mutants — a new Apocrypha and Pseudepigrapha. The novelists of depravity, the enthusiastic college instructors, the unqualified "teams" of sex-therapists, the smut salesmen who appear in court as the champions of free speech and free press — all the preachers of permissiveness — these are its priests and prophets; the casual and "cool' approach, its official theology; the inhibitions of traditional morality, its Devil; the stream of heavily annotated statistical studies of the breakdown of sexual morality, the documented "proof" of the truth of its revelation; the unmarried state of maximum bisexual opportunities and unrestrained scatology, its eschatological vision.

But alas, this New Dispensation is not new at all. The psychological veneer and the existentialist vernacular may indeed be novel; but the underlying theories are those of the old paganism that expressed itself in a variety of ways, from the sacred prostitution of Canaan to the ribald debauchery of Rome. The irresistibility of the primal urge and the absolute sanctity of pleasure were not at all unknown to the ancient world.

The "new morality" is the old hedonistic immorality in a new and appealing guise.

This is the prevailing sentiment of the environment in which most of us live. It is, one must grant, not totally reprehensible. It has contributed an element of integrity and frankness to our discussion and understanding of sex and its role in our lives, and this honesty has happily helped us get rid of some of the heavy-handed sanctimoniousness that used to characterize our talk — or refusal to talk — about sex. But for the greatest part, this renaissance of paganism represents the most serious threat, in centuries, to morality — and hence to the family unit and, ultimately, to man himself. The disintegration of the family and the fragmentation of man are not one bit less of a mortal peril to the future of mankind than the splitting of the atom. And our very unprudish openness and frankness about matters sexual has served to push deeper into the unconscious the very antithesis of this whole approach to sex: a puritanical, ascetic, sex-negating outlook that is as real as it is denied.

This anti-sexual notion is, in the truest sense of the word, reactionary: it was, historically, a reaction to the excesses of paganism's unbridled sexual laxity. Early Christianity identified sex as the original sin, and considered the act of procreation as that which transmits sin from one generation to the other. The founders of Christianity recommended celibacy and considered marriage as but a concession to man's weakness; it is better, they taught, to marry than to burn (with passion). It is not enough to control the sexual urge; one must, if possible, repress it completely. Christianity has, through the centuries, struggled with this profoundly negative attitude towards sex, born of the disgust with the permissiveness and sex-glorification of the ancient pagan world. Both opposing views can be traced to the same origin, Gnosticism (See Hans Jonas, *The Gnostic Religion*).

Despite the fact that this attitude apparently commands no allegiance from the contemporary mind, and suggests nothing more than antiquarian interest, its roots strike deep into the psyche of most of us. Christianity is one of the major sources of Western civilization, and this Augustinian philosophy of sex has retained a residual hold on the mind of Western man by going underground; it leads a subterranean life all its own despite our overt contradiction of its claims and principles. Psychologists are aware of the pathological consequences of this aversion to, and fear of, sex, especially in a society which ostensibly espouses an attitude diametrically opposed to it. Most of us will recognize its presence in our own mental constitution without it necessarily appearing as an illness or aberration. Some tend, inwardly, to consider sex as "dirty" and salacious, as something which belongs in the gutter, but is, by a kind of official hypocrisy, legitimized in the marital chamber. If this is putting the case somewhat harshly, it is only to emphasize a fact that runs counter to the generally accepted, "healthy" view of sex.

Body and Soul

Judaism denies both extremes. It rejects paganism's fulsome espousal of uninhibited sexual expression, and denies, with equal vehemence, Christianity's begrudging concept of marriage and its condemnation of all sexual activity as inherently sinful. *Giluy arayot* or unchastity is considered one of the three cardinal sins, such that man must surrender his life in order to avoid transgressing them. However, it is only illegitimate sexual congress that is deemed sinful and *to'evah*, abominable; no such stigma is ever attached to sex in general. "The soul is Thine and the body is Thine," and there is no reason to denigrate the needs of the body while cherishing the demands of the soul. "The *Shechinah* (Divine Presence) dwells in a home," the Kabbalah teaches, "only when a man is married and he cohabits with his wife."[1] The commandment to propagate the race is the first ever given to man. While sex is, indeed, a natural physical function, and of such immense power that none is exempt from the blandishments of sexual temptation, it is the means whereby God's world is populated

---

1 Zohar, I, 122a.

and the divine will, executed; hence, it is a sacred instrument.[2]

Moreover, sexual comradeship is an intrinsic good, beyond the demands of procreation. In the Bible's first account of the creation of man, in which he is presented as essentially a natural creature, he is immediately commanded to be fruitful and multiply and rule over all the rest of nature — the instinctive urges of sex and power (Gen. 1: 26-28). However, in the second and more detailed account, where the moral nature of man is elaborated, there is no mention of propagation. Instead, "And the Lord God said, it is not good that man should be alone. I will make a help meet for him.... Therefore shall a man leave his father and

---

2 This thesis is interestingly advocated in the 13th century *Iggereth Hakodesh*, parts of which are translated in my *The Good Society: Jewish Ethics in Action* (Viking Press, 1974), chapter 9.

his mother and cleave to his wife and they shall become one flesh" (Gen. 2: 18-25).[3] The loving companionship of husband and wife is an end in itself, a virtue sanctioned and sanctified by the Creator. "It is not good that man should be alone" — man's inner capacity for goodness can never be realized unless he has a mate upon whom to shower his selfless affection.[4]

Throughout the Halakhah (Jewish Law) we find this Jewish view of sex forcefully expressed. Judaism's uncompromising strictures on adultery, for instance, are sufficiently well-known and a good indication of its abhorrence of proscribed sexual relations. The ability to practice restraint in the

---

3 On the profound differences between the two accounts of man's creation, see Rabbi Joseph B. Soloveitchik's "The Lonely Man of Faith," *Tradition* (Summer, 1965).

4 Cf. R. Yaakov Zevi Meklenburg. *Ha-Ketav ve-ha-Kabbalah,* to Gen. 1:4.

presence of temptation — and Judaism was immensely realistic in its assessment of man's vulnerability to sexual desire — is an expression of holiness. That is why the Biblical portion listing the prohibited relationships is read publicly in the synagogue on the afternoon of Yom Kippur — for the holiest day of the year is appropriate to the study of that which, if observed, leads man to the self-transcendence called holiness. At the same time, as indicated, within the limits set by the Torah's morality, the sexual bond is not only tolerated but affirmed and encouraged. Sexual communion is considered a legal right of the wife, no less than the food and clothing her husband is required to provide for her. And, once again, this view of the sexual relationship is essentially independent of the question — important in its own right — of procreation; therefore sexual activity is not at all prohibited when it cannot lead to child-bearing, such as for those who have passed the menopause or are sterile or pregnant.[5]

Under the wedding canopy itself, among the seven blessings recited at the occasion of marriage, we bless God Who "created man in His image" and formed him so as to perpetuate himself. According to the Torah, God imprinted this dual nature in man without considering it an inner contradiction. "And God created the man in His image. . . male and female created He them. And God blessed them, and God said unto them, be fruitful and multiply. . ." (Gen. 1: 27, 28). The divine image and sexuality

---

[5] This is in direct opposition to certain sects (such as the Essenes, as described by the historian Josephus), contemporaries of the Rabbis of the Mishnah, which prohibited connubial intercourse **during** pregnancy. **Similar attitudes prevailed** among related sects. See Dr. Menahem M. Brayer's article in *Harofe Haivri,* Vol. 38 (1965) pp. 151-160.

are not antonyms. To possess a soul and to beget children are not an inconsistency, a flaw in creation, a divine oversight. The Jew finds no lasting antagonism in the encounter between man's divine image and his sexual nature, between body and soul. If these two — man's spiritual nature with its self-restraint and moral demands, and his sexual nature with its grasping urges — are in conflict, the contradiction is only apparent, not fundamental.

Image and Instinct:
The Resolution

It is at the occasion of one's marriage that the exalted teachings of the Torah on sex become most germane and most cogent for the Jew and Jewess. Before this great day in their lives, bride and groom had to overpower their inner sexual demands by exerting their moral natures. The contest within each of them was a difficult, intense one. As in any struggle, hostility is engendered — whether or not the moral side was successful in its engagement with the physical. Guilt is the means by which the moral nature of man seeks to subdue the sexual, and by which sexual victory is robbed of the joy of its conquests.

But this opposition is an ephemeral one. In marriage the divine image and the divinely created sexual instinct are reconciled. At this time when, with the sanction and blessing of the Almighty, one's spiritual-moral character and one's sexual-physical existence are to be harmonized, and their conflicts resolved, it is most urgent to enter the wedding relationship in a state of moral purity and equanimity. Any attitude brought to the marital chamber that, consciously or unconsciously, regards sex as evil and identifies desire with lust, can only disturb the harmonious integration of the two forces within man: the moral and the sexual. For there is no real, intrinsic contradiction between them; sex is not, in and of itself, when legitimately expressed, sinful or salacious or beastly or deserving of guilt. Before husband and wife can "become one flesh," each has to be integrated within himself and herself. Without this inner peace, the stilling of the early turmoil and conflict, the two separate individuals should hardly be expected to attain conjugal concord. Before they are joined to each other, therefore, bride and groom must purge themselves of any notions about the physical expression of love that might prove injurious to a full, wholesome relationship.

It is precisely this that Family Purity achieves for the young couple about to be married, and, thereafter, throughout their married life together.

First, however, we must state exactly what Family Purity entails.

What Is It?

It is Judaism's pride that it is more than just a religion. Its concerns are not limited to formulating dogma or prescribing official ceremonies or organizing public worship. Its judgments embrace every area of significance in the life of man — from his business practices to his daily diet, his leisure pursuits to his filial obligations, his social demeanor to his historical memory, his metaphysical yearnings to the way he dresses. It is, in fact, this very breadth of its interests that is at once its glory and its chief obstacle, for people are wont to look with suspicion and impatience upon whatever refuses to yield to predetermined classifications and well defined categories.

The Halakhah (Jewish Law) has a great

deal to say about the sexual conduct of married couples. Sex certainly is not the only ingredient in married life, maybe not even the most important. But it surely is of sufficient significance and consequence for the Halakhah to treat it with the utmost gravity and seriousness. Marriage and the problems related to it form a significant part of the entire Talmudic literature. Over one-sixth of the Talmud itself, one whole "Order," is devoted to such matters as marriage, divorce, and women's rights. Every area of married life, bar none, is discussed in the Talmud with the greatest delicacy, but always forthrightly and without either prudery or sentimentalism. Of special importance are the sexual aspects of marriage, to which the Talmud devotes a full tractate, called *Niddah*, in addition to lengthy passages in other tractates.

It is not the purpose of this essay to describe these laws in detail. Its essentials are necessary, however, in order for the reader to appreciate the multifaceted divine wisdom that inheres in them. Jewish Law forbids a husband to approach his wife during the time of her menses, generally from five to seven days, and extends the prohibition of any physical contact beyond this period for another seven days, known as the "seven clean days." (That is why one will find two beds in observant Jewish homes, or at least a couch for the husband during this period.) During this time husband and wife are expected to act towards each other with respect and affection but without any physical expression of love — excellent training for the time, later in their lives, when husband and wife will have to discover bonds other than sex to link them one to another.[6]

---

6 Cf. Commentary of R. Samson Raphael Hirsch to Lev. 20:18.

At the end of this twelve to fourteen day period (depending upon the individual woman), the menstruant (known as *niddah*) must immerse herself in a body of water known as a *mikvah* and recite a special blessing in which she praises God for sanctifying us with His commandments and commanding us concerning immersion (*tevillah*).

The *mikvah* itself — along with its prescribed dimensions and source of the water — is an ancient institution. Ordained by the Bible, it was in wide use during the times of the two Temples; one who had contracted any of the various kinds of "impurity" was forbidden to eat of sacrificial meat or the tithe, or to enter the precincts of the Temple. The way of effecting purification was through immersion in the *mikvah*. Most of these forms of impurity have fallen into disuse today, simply because of the historical circumstance of the destruction of the Temple in 70 C.E.; today there is neither sacrifice nor Temple. Only the law of impurity of *niddah* remains intact, for it affects not only the right to enter the Temple in Jerusalem, but also the intimate marital relationship of every couple. (One might add, as a historical note, that Christianity took over from Judaism the institution of *tevillah,* or immersion, as the rite of initiation into the Christian communion; but that in the course of time it modified it so that most sects define baptism as the sprinkling of water upon the communicant rather than full immersion in the pool.) *Mikvah* is used today not only for Family Purity, but also for the initiation of proselytes, both male and female, into Judaism, and for immersing certain kinds of new household vessels. In addition, some pious male Jews immerse themselves before prayer and before Sabbaths and Holy Days. The *mikvah* is a communal institution, generally an inconspicuous building, and administered with the utmost modesty and delicacy, often luxuriously appointed.

Discarding the Relics

By thus preparing for their wedding, and afterwards for their monthly marital reunion — separating from each other and then, before joining each other, the wife immersing in the *mikvah* and reciting thereupon the blessing thanking the Almighty for sanctifying us through this institution — husband and wife acknowledge, in the most profound symbolic manner, that their relationship is sanctified and blessed, that it is pure and not vulgar, sacred and not salacious. Family Purity has a magnificent cleansing effect upon the psyche. It purifies and ennobles the outlook of man and woman upon each other and their relationship to each other. The very waters of the *mikvah* seem to wash away any fallacious, psychologically damaging thoughts which, carryovers from youth, may well imperil the mutual love and respect that alone can keep a home stable. *Mikvah* becomes the sacred instrumentality whereby morality and sexuality are reconciled, bringing husband and wife to each other in purity and delicacy, their love undefiled by the guilt and shame that are the relics of obsolete inner struggles.

No philosophy of sex, no matter how well and cogently articulated, can ever be as psychologically meaningful and compelling as the observance of Family Purity. Only the actual practice of these laws can successfully inculcate Judaism's values and insights into this immensely significant and delicate area of life.

II.

A Spiritual Institution

In order to appreciate the implications of Family Purity, it is important to understand, as well, what it is *not*.

No Superstition

For one thing, it is not the kind of superstition that, in other cultures, has stigmatized the menstruant as repulsive, placed upon her mysterious and stringent taboos, and banished her from the community for the duration of her menses. Maimonides, the eminent twelfth century Talmudist, philosopher, and physician, forcefully rejected the superstitious beliefs and practices of the

Sabeans, Magi, and other Eastern peoples concerning menstruation, and emphasized the spiritual content of Judaism's teachings.[1] The Torah's legislation is simply not of one piece with, for instance, the primitive customs recorded in Sir James Frazer's *The Golden Bough*. Unfortunately, such identification of the Torah's laws with primitive pagan and mythological cultures often does take place in the mind of the contemporary Jew or Jewess who is uninitiated into the world of Torah and the Jewish Tradition and who cannot, therefore, view Jewish Family Purity from a broader perspective and greater knowledgeability. A terminological confusion is largely responsible for this unhappy distortion of the Torah's larger purposes and the intrinsic meaning of its

---

[1] Maimonides, *Guide to the Perplexed*, Part III, Chap. 47.

commandments. *Taharah* and *tum'ah* (and the corresponding adjectives *tahor* and *tamei*) are usually translated as "pure" and "impure." It is this deceptive semantic delinquency that leads to the interpretation of these categories as denoting some kind of intrinsic mysterious abhorrence that possesses the person of the menstruant and that must be purged by some magical incantation.

But this is clearly not so. According to Jewish teaching, nothing whatever happens to or changes in the person or character or value of the individual, man or woman, designated as "impure." No special quality makes such an individual inferior, in any way, to any other person referred to as "pure." The terms *taharah* and *tum'ah* signify *halakhic* or legal categories. They merely indicate that certain patterns of behavior become obligatory in each case. Hence the

Halakhah does not regard it as incumbent upon or meritorious for one who is "impure" to achieve the state of being "pure"; it merely declares that in this state of "impurity" one may not, as has been previously mentioned, partake of sacred food, i.e., sacrifices and priestly tithes, or enter the grounds of the Sanctuary. If, in the case of *niddah*, the Halakhah does consider it a virtue for the woman to immerse herself and regain the state of "purity" (*tevillah bi'zemanah mitzvah*), it is only because it regards the resumption of full conjugal relationships without undue delay as contributing to the fulfillment of one of the major purposes of marriage.

A Semantic Tragedy

There is another and even more widespread popular misconception of the nature of Family Purity that has served to subvert its observance by many Jews. This, too, is largely the result of a mistranslation, and is nothing less than a semantic tragedy. The terms *taharah* and *tum'ah* have been rendered as "cleanliness" and "uncleanliness." No wonder that so many young people reject the whole institution offhand: certainly in this scientific age, with our technological progress in hygiene and sanitation, we do not need to abide by ancient ritual regulations in order to keep clean!

Let it therefore be stated decisively and unequivocally: Family Purity is *not* just a hygienic procedure. *"Tum'ah* is not a kind of adhesion or dirt that is washed off by water; it is a decree of Scripture, and it has to do with the intention in one's heart."[2]

---

2 Maimonides, Laws of *Mikvaot,* 11:12.

The injunction to keep one's body clean and one's physique healthy is regarded in Judaism as a virtue in and of and by itself, separate from the other laws. It should not be confused, as people sometimes unwittingly do, with the purposes of any other commandments. Thus, for instance, the High Priest during the days of the Temple had to undergo five immersions during the Yom Kippur services. Certainly, considering the form of worship which he conducted, one ought not to suspect the High Priest of having so soiled himself that he required five baths for hygienic purposes! Quite evidently, the function of immersion is something other than hygienic. Indeed, the Halakhah requires the *niddah* to be thoroughly clean *before* immersion!

In this connection, it should be noted that some writers have observed that Family Purity results in imposing medical benefits, especially relating to the incidence of certain kinds of cancer. But more impressive is the fact that this cycle of abstention and fulfillment provides for a recovery period for both husband and wife, one which establishes a much-needed regulation of the sexual rhythm of the male as well as the female, and allows for a replenishment of the libidinal reservoir. No voluntary separation can ever be as effective in providing this relaxation as one which is mutually accepted as religiously binding, and in which neither spouse may approach the other and, therefore, where neither need fear to decline and have his or her affection or fidelity suspect.

Yet this, too, must not be mistaken for the purpose of these laws or as exhausting their full significance. Family Purity is a profoundly *spiritual*, *religious* institution. It may have (as it most certainly does) far-reaching psychological implications and beneficial physical consequences; but the appreciation of the meaning of these laws simply does not belong in the province of the psychologist or physician, or of the anthropologist or sanitary engineer.

*Beyond
Prayer
and Study*

It is difficult to convey adequately the over-riding importance Judaism places upon these laws, especially to a generation that is largely ignorant of their existence. Perhaps the best measure of their significance lies in the punishment that the Torah prescribes for their violation — *karet* (excision, being cut off from the people of Israel), the same as that for transgressing the Yom Kippur fast! Moreover, the sense of the Law assigns priority to Family Purity over public prayer and Torah reading; hence if a community cannot afford to erect all three communal structures, the building of the *mikvah* takes precedence over the building of the Synagogue and the writing of the Scroll of the Torah. The purity of the Jewish family, more than worship by the community or the pursuit of scholarship, is responsible for the perpetuation of the House of Israel.

The reader must not accept the sketch of the laws of Family Purity, presented above, as by any means adequate for the purpose of proper observance. As in all other areas of the Halakhah — and in all of life! — it is the details that determine the success of the whole venture; only the attention one pays to the particulars gives meaning to the underlying principles. For these detailed laws one may refer to the *Shulhan Arukh*, the Code of Jewish Law, or to any of the popular translations of its digests. Even better, the following booklets may be consulted:

1. Maurice Lamm, *The Jewish Way in Love and Marriage*, published by Harper & Row, N.Y.

2. Aryeh Kaplan, *Waters of Eden*, published by the National Council of Synagogue Youth (NCSY / UOJCA), N.Y.

3. Reuven Bulka, *Jewish Marriage*, published by Ktav, Hoboken N.J.

4. Eliahu Kitov, *The Jew and His Home*, trans. Nathan Bulman, Published by Shengold, New York.

5. Zev Schostak, *A Guide to Jewish Family Laws*, published by Feldheim, New York.

A brief resumé of these laws is included in Chapter VI of this volume.

Flavor Added

What is attempted in the present work belongs in the category of *taamei ha-mitzvot*, the explanations of the commandments. By this is meant not an endeavor to discover God's reasons for His laws, for that is well nigh impossible and, moreover, an act of presumption and intellectual arrogance by man. Rather, to borrrow a dichotomy proposed by Dr. Samuel Belkin, President of Yeshiva University, we are attempting to fathom the *purposes* (as opposed to *reasons*) inherent and implicit in the commandments and precepts. In other words, we want to know not why God commanded them, but what He wanted us to learn from them, i.e., the function of the commandments in the larger horizons of our life. It is, of course, understood that taken in this light the laws are independent of the purposes we find in them. For a law to be a law, it must be autonomous, and not contingent upon our rationalizations. *"Taamei ha-mitzvot"* means literally, "the tastes of the commandments";

the translation "reasons" is derivative. It is in this sense that we here undertake the search for the larger ends of the laws of Family Purity. By inquiring into our religious institutions for their relevant purposes, we seek to add delightful and satisfying flavor to our spiritual diet; but by no means may we substitute the "taste" for the substance of our religious foods, namely, the actual precepts of Judaism carried out in practice. Throughout our history there have been those who attempted to do just that, subordinating the laws to the reasons they presumed to discover for them; but such spiritual gourmets have ultimately starved and withered. The Law must remain independent of and unconditioned by the values, reasons, and purposes we believe we have found in it.

III.

Staying Married

That Judaism's view of these most intimate aspects of married life is worthy of
consideration by modern young couples is
indicated by the striking record of domestic
happiness characteristic of Orthodox Jewish
homes even in the midst of an environment
where the breakdown of family life becomes
more shocking with each year. After de-
scribing the felicity that has distinguished
the observant Jewish family since the Middle
Ages, a noted Reform leader writes:

> Particularly in those households where Or-
> thodox Judaism is practiced and observed —·
> both in Europe and in cosmopolitan American
> centers — almost the entire rubric we have

drawn of Jewish home life in the Middle Ages may be observed even today. In those homes where the liberties of Emancipation have infiltrated there exists a wide variety of family patterns, conditioned by the range of defection from Orthodox tradition. . .

It was possible for a historian, viewing the whole of the present-day Jewish scene, to say, only a few years ago, "The family possesses more than ordinary importance in Jewish life, for it is the bond of cohesion which has safeguarded the purity of the race and the continuity of religious tradition. It is the stronghold of Jewish sentiment, in which Jewish life unfolds itself in its most typical forms and intimate phases." This is certainly true of those families in which concern for religious tradition exists, even in most unorthodox expression. . .[1]

This typical Jewish family cohesion is surely not the result of any indigenous ethnic

---

[1] Stanley R. Brav, *Marriage and the Jewish Tradition* (New York: Philosophical Library, 1951), p. 98f.

or racial virtue of the Jewish people. Nor does it derive from some general, well-intentioned but amorphous "concern for religious tradition." It is, most certainly, the product of the specific "Orthodox" tradition — the Halakhah or Jewish "way of life." It is this codified tradition, this obligatory Law, that has bestowed the gift of stability upon the Jewish family.

The Jewish "Way"

There are, no doubt, many elements among those that constitute the halakhic "way" that, together, strengthen the fabric of Jewish family life. But there can be little doubt that foremost among them is that body of laws that treats directly of conjugal relations. The code prescribed by Jewish Law for husband and wife is generally referred to as *taharat hamishpahah*, "the purity of the family." It is, as we have already seen, a most appropriate euphemism, for it addresses itself to the aspiration for that form of self-transcendence known as *taharah* or purity, and provides marvelous and magnificent safeguards for the integrity of the *mishpahah* or family.

We have discussed above the sense of psychological purification that is attained by observance of immersion in the *mikvah* by the bride. But the psychological implications of Family Purity are not restricted to the general nature of sex as it expresses itself in the early years of marriage. *Taharat ha-mishpahah* is also crucial in protecting the marital bond from one of its most universal and perilous enemies which comes to the fore soon after the newness of married life has worn off: the tendency for sex to become routinized.

It is easy enough to get married. It is quite another thing to stay married. The Talmud considers the pairing of couples as difficult as the splitting of the waters of the Red Sea; and the miracle there was not so much the separation of the waters as the keeping them apart so that the Exodus might proceed successfully. So with the joining of husband and wife. The *wedding*, for all the problems it presents to the young couple and their families, is comparatively simple. Far more significant, far more difficult, and a far greater miracle to achieve in this turbulent society is — the *marriage*, staying married.

Sexual attraction plays a major role in bringing a man and woman to the bridal canopy, and keeping the couple together in the early months and years of marriage. But if this attraction wanes and withers in the years following, the permanence of the marriage itself is imperiled and may likewise slowly disintegrate.

So often—so unfortunately! — that is exactly what happens. What to the young, recently married couple is such an exciting and fulfilling adventure, soon becomes just another dull experience to be re-enacted almost mechanically as part of the whole marital complex. The charm and the delight, the thrill and the beauty of young love is soon replaced by the stale and the prosaic, the plain and the profane. There is hardly a more deadly poison that so threatens the existence of a happy marriage!

Familiarity and Boredom

For marriage to thrive, the attractiveness of wife and husband for each other that prevailed during the early period of the marriage must be preserved and even enhanced. And it is the abstinence enjoined by Family Purity that helps keep that attraction and longing fresh and youthful. This is how the Talmud explained the psychological ramifications of *taharat ha-mishpahah*:

> Because a man may become over-acquainted with [his wife] and thus repelled by her, therefore the Torah said that she should be considered a *niddah* for seven days, i.e., after the end of her period, so that she might become beloved of her husband on the day of her purification even as she was on the day of her marriage. [2]

Unrestricted approachability leads to over-indulgence. And this over-familiarity, with its consequent satiety and boredom and *ennui*, is a direct and powerful cause of marital disharmony. When, however, the couple follows the Torah's sexual disci-

---

[2] *Niddah,* 31b.

pline and observes this period of separation, the ugly spectre of over-fulfillment and habituation is banished and the refreshing zest of early love is ever-present.

There is so much insight in this comment of the Rabbis! Familiarity does indeed breed contempt, and a little absence does make the heart grow fonder. As Chief Rabbi Unterman of Israel has pointed out, it has been the experience of people who deal in marriage counselling that sometimes a husband will ask for a legal separation on the way to divorce. Then, after he has been separated a while from his wife, he suddenly discovers that he needs her and wants her and even loves her! The separation is a prelude to reunion. This separation, too, which Judaism commands as part of the observance of Family Purity, is that which puts the poetry back into marriage, which retains the charm, the elegance, the excitement. It is the pause that refreshes all, of married life.

A Perpetual Honeymoon

Moreover, Family Purity has an additional benefit, especially for the woman: it preserves the beauty of the early months of marriage. Men usually do not appreciate this as do women, for sex is relatively extraneous to the inner life of a man, whereas it is an integral part of a woman's being. One hesitates, in this day of Women's Lib, to repeat that "biology is destiny," but certainly biology is more profoundly a part of psychology for a woman than for a man. During the time that a little boy thinks of a career as a soldier or fireman, or as a doctor or a scientist, the little girl, even if she aspires to a profession or business career, still principally dreams of marriage and family and home, of children and domestic life. As she grows older, her attention is progressively more devoted to her dreams of engagement and marriage, her visions of love and affection. The culmination of her dreams comes with the period of engagement, when she is courted and wooed by her fiance. Then there is the climax of the wedding night and the honeymoon, and the being together thereafter ("and they shall be unto one flesh").

What a pity if this rapturous realization of her dreams should come and go, departing for ever after! What a cruel and frustrating experience if a week or a month should spell the complete fulfillment of a lifetime of lovely ambitions and delightful aspirations! With the institution of *taharat ha-mishpaḥah*, however, a marvelous domestic miracle occurs: the honeymoon lasts throughout the greatest part of one's active life! The drama of love-without-sexual-contact followed by the loving union of husband and wife and their being together is repeated every month. Thus, the separation of husband and wife physically during the period of *niddah* and the "seven clean days," when they may express to each other feelings of tenderness without any physical contact, is equivalent to the period of engagement. Then, just as she did when she was a bride, the wife undergoes the immersion in a *mikvah*, recites the same blessing she did as a bride, and comes to her husband, in purity and love, as she did on her wedding night.

Love does not grow stale in such an environment. A young woman's dreams remain fresh, her visions vital, and her hopes radiant throughout life. All of life presents the opportunity of becoming a perpetual honeymoon. Her dreams are not defeated by success and frustrated by fulfillment.

Civilizing Sex

There is yet a third psychological consequence of Family Purity that is deserving of attention. *Taharat ha-mishpaḥah* has a profound influence upon the way husband and wife view each other. Modern philosophers and social thinkers, inspired by Martin Buber, speak of the two ways in which we may approach our fellow human beings: as a "thou" or as an "it." The first is the way we relate to another human being as a subject and a person, a vital, independent, autonomous being possessed of dignity and inner value. The second way is the viewing of another human being as an object, one devoid of values and selfhood, a "thing," an instrument to manipulate for the satisfaction of my goals, my ends, my purposes. In the first instance, I meet and confront another human being; in the second, I use or abuse him or her as mere chattel.

Unquestionably, a sexual relationship inclines towards an "I-It" rather than an "I-Thou" relationship. There is a tendency to regard the sexual partner as a "thing," as an object for the fulfillment of one's own passions and desires. The cave-man who pulled his mate by her hair (it may be a caricature, but the type persists today!) did not view her as a *person* of inner dignity; she was an object like other objects in his life. Perhaps, to be truthful, it is inevitable that this objectification must remain to some extent a part of one's basic sexual orientation. Yet, even if we should concede that it must exist in some measure, we must not allow it to get out of hand lest it become dehumanizing. Such an attitude destroys the dignity of the individual — both the individual so viewed and the one who does the viewing. If it is permitted to develop to the point where one's mate is considered only

64

an object for the fulfillment of one's desires, then there is a very real danger that it will carry over into every other aspect of life. Such a fundamental psychological orientation cannot be contained in the bedroom—it must spread its nefarious influence into every nook and corner of one's existence. The brute within man is civilized in proportion to the degree that he regards his fellow-man, and especially his mate, as a "thou" rather than an "it."

It is here that *taharat ha-mishpaḥah* exerts a most beneficent influence over the inner-most depths of the psyches of husband and wife. By restraining the husband from pursuing his sexual goals in uncontrolled fashion, it informs him, in the most potent manner possible, that his wife was not created only for his pleasure. When the husband, in mutual commitment with his wife to the higher visions of Judaism, accepts the institution of Family Purity—and he recognizes that no matter how overpowering his passions, how persuasive his proposals, and how willing or unwilling his wife, he must refrain from approaching her in any manner whatever—he realizes in the very depths of his being that she is a person who possesses inner worth, autonomous value, and sacred and inalienable rights at least equal to his own. Were she but a thing, an object, he could do with her as he pleases, within limits set only by his persuasiveness or, even worse, his superior physical prowess. By following the Halakhah, however, a husband learns, slowly and gradually, but surely and firmly, that his wife is human, that she is endowed with divine dignity, that she is a "thou" and not an "it," that she is a person and not a thing.

There are some people who imagine that voluntary separation will accomplish the same result, and that it is therefore unnecessary to follow the whole pattern laid down by Jewish Law. But such voluntary separation ultimately proves inadequate. One partner may suspect coldness on the part of the one who proposes the withdrawal. Moreover, a lack of religious sanction means that the entire separation will no longer be elevating and ennobling as it can be only when it is informed by religious significance.

So necessary and beneficial are the psychological consequences of Family Purity, so profound and far-reaching is its judgment and influence over the nature of marriage and the institution of married life, that if it did not exist already, we should have to invent it for our own protection and welfare. "Happy are we — how good is our destiny, how pleasant our lot, how beautiful our heritage" (*The Prayer Book*).

IV.

The Sanctity of Time

The enormous importance of Family Purity may be appreciated in the context of a fundamental principle involving the duties and obligations of women in Jewish Law. Viewed in this manner, it will be seen to possess significance that far transcends its place as an individual *mitzvah* within the context of the 613 biblical commandments.

The Woman's Obligations

Jewish Law does not require of women the same extent of observance that it does of men. Whereas men are obligated to observe all the 613 biblical commandments,

68

and the many more rabbinic ordinances, women are excused from observing certain of these precepts. The criterion of observance is based upon the classification of the commandments. All negative commandments, "thou shalt not," are equally obligatory upon men and women.[1] With the positive commandments, "thou shalt," however, we distinguish between those commandments that are applicable at all times, or regardless of any specific time, and those that are conditioned by time, i.e., the time when it is to be observed is an integral feature in the precept itself. Thus, for instance, the prohibition against eating non-kosher food, or lying, or stealing, or gossiping, or refraining from eating on Yom Kippur, because these are negative command-

---

[1] There are three exceptions; v. Mishnah *Kiddushin* 29a.

ments, fall equally upon men and women. Positive commandments such as the *mitzvah* to love God or to fear Him, or to honor one's parents, because such precepts apply at all times, are again equally obligatory upon male and female. However, such time-oriented positive precepts as the sounding of the *shofar* (on Rosh Hashanah), or eating in the *sukkah* (on Sukkot), or laying the *tefillin* (only during day-time), are obligatory only upon men (insofar as the Halakhah is concerned; by *minhag*, or custom, women have generally accepted certain *mitzvot* such as *shofar* and *lulav*).

This criterion is fundamental to the whole structure of Halakhah insofar as it affects the standards of observance demanded of men and of women. What is the rationale for this particular distinction? Many answers have been offered. The most popular is that which was proposed by a late medieval sage, Abudrahm, who avers that the Torah appreciates a woman's obligations to her household, and regards it as an inordinate demand upon her if she be held responsible to keep those commandments that are limited to specific times. Therefore, since her duties towards her household are primary, she is excused from such commandments that must be performed only at certain times or seasons; all other commandments, however, are binding upon her.

Whether this explanation is sufficient or not is irrelevant for the purpose of this essay. What is here proposed is another explanation which goes much deeper and strikes much more profoundly at the Torah's conception of the respective natures of men and women and, consequently, their obligations to observe the Torah. In order to understand it, it is first necessary to ask ourselves, even before we consider the question of women's observance: what, after all, is the benefit of the commandments whose observance is limited to the calendar or clock? What *inherent* difference is there between time-oriented commandments and those which are timeless?

Two Types of Holiness

The answer necessitates a distinction between two types of holiness: the holiness of time and the holiness of place, the latter term comprehending also the holiness of objects, which have extension and hence occupy space.

Judaism has great regard for the holiness of place. For instance, a synagogue is a holy place. The Land of Israel is the "Holy Land." The city of Jerusalem has an even higher degree of sanctity than the Land of Israel, and the Mount of the Temple even more than the rest of Jerusalem. The Inner Sanctum is the holiest place on earth. Or, with regard to objects, a properly written *Sefer Torah* is considered holy. Of derivative sanctity is the printed Pentateuch or the Talmud or any other "holy book."

Yet the holiness of time is far more comprehensive and compelling. The holiness of time includes not only the Sabbath and the "holy days," but also various times within the profane days which can be *made* holy: if the daytime is reserved for prayer and *tefillin*, and the nighttime for a different type of prayer or a different type of *mitzvah*, then they are, accordingly, sanctified by our performance of these various precepts.

The holiness of time, the awareness of the sacredness of history, is the first type of *kedushah* mentioned in the Bible. Immediately after the creation of man on the sixth day, his first experience was that of the holiness of time: the Sabbath.[2] "And the Lord blessed the seventh day and He sanctified it" (Gen. 2: 3). One can go through all of life without ever coming into contact with a holy place or a holy object. But, if he lives more than a single week, he has already been subject to the holiness of time.[3]

The holiness of space impinges upon our consciousness and inspires reverence within

---

[2] Although the Sabbath is the archetype of the holiness of time, women too are required to observe it because the Torah's Law of the Sabbath is both positive (to sanctify it, i.e., recite the *Kiddush*) and negative (not to perform labor). Women, as has been mentioned, must observe all the negative precepts as must men, and since they are thus obliged to keep the Sabbath, their obligation extends to *Kiddush* as well.

[3] It has been suggested that circumcision was ordained by the Torah for the eighth day so as to make sure that every child will have experienced at least one holy day before entering into the Covenant of Abraham. See *Avodat Yisrael*, to *Emor*, by the Ḥasidic Ẓaddik R. Israel of Kozenitz.

is only when we encounter that place or object designated as holy. The holiness of time sanctifies every moment of life. It makes us aware of the fact that every minute is pregnant with possibilities of divine significance. The challenge of the holiness of time pursues us incessantly; it will not let us rest in the profaneness of insignificance. We can avoid certain circumscribed geographical areas; we can never escape recurrent periods in history. We may be exiled from a holy place; we never are alienated from a holy time. When Israel was exiled from the Holy Land, it was banished from contact with the holiest of places. But it took along with it, to all corners of the world, the resources for the holiness of time: the commandments of the Torah.

The *mitzvot* make us aware of these two types of holiness. The commandments relating to the Land of Israel, or to the synagogue or the Temple or sacred objects, enhance the principle of the holiness of place. The laws relating to Sabbath and Festivals remind us of the holiness of time. And, most significant, each and every precept which is geared to time, whether time of the day or season of the year, inspires us to attain the higher holiness, that of time. Without these commandments, a human being might never be aware of this spiritual quality of the holiness of time — and time is the story of existence itself.

Man urgently needs these time-oriented commandments so that he thereby be made aware of the sanctity of time.

The Inner Rhythm

However, this holds true only for males. Women are excused from observing these commandments for the simple reason that they *do not need them*. A woman does not

76

need the time-conditioned commandments, because she is already aware of the sanctification of time in a manner far more profound, far more intimate and personal, and far more convincing than that which a man can attain by means of the extraneous observances which he is commanded. For a woman, unlike a man, has a built-in biological clock. The periodicity of her menses implies an inner biological rhythm that forms part and parcel of her life. If this inner rhythm is not sanctified, she never attains the sanctity of time. But if she observes the laws of Family Purity, then she has, by virtue of observing this one *mitzvah*, geared her inner clock, her essential periodicity, to an act of holiness.[4] By the observ-

---

[4] This thought has been suggested by Rabbi Emanuel Rackman, *Tradition* (vol. I, no. 1). Cf. MaHaRaL (R. Loewe of Prague), *Derush al Ha-mitzvot*, page 30.

ance of this single commandment she is made conscious of the holiness of time to an extent far more comprehensive than that attained by a man. A woman, therefore, does not *need* the time-oriented commandments to remind her of the holiness of time;[5] whereas a man, who does not possess this inner periodicity, must rely upon these many commandments to summon him to the sanctification of time.

The laws of Family Purity are, therefore, a divine gift to woman, allowing her to attain this highest of all forms of sanctity. Her responsiveness to history — the arena where God makes His will manifest and where man confronts his Maker — is internal, not external.

---

[5] This principle holds true for woman*kind*, and therefore applies to all women irrespective of marital status or physical condition, i.e. after menopause as well.

V.

The Affirmation of Life

The institution of Family Purity possesses grand symbolic significance when seen in the context of all of the Torah's legislation concerning *tum'ah* and *taharah*, terms which are loosely and misleadingly translated as "uncleanliness" and "cleanliness" or "purity" and "impurity." The reason we term these translations inaccurate is because they imply, or at least they allow the listener to infer, that there is some hygienic element involved in them. This, of course, as explained above, is simply not so. They are spiritual states, and have no relation to physical disgust or attractiveness. For want of better words, however, we shall retain the Hebrew or keep the terms "pure" and "impure."

The laws of *taharah* and *tum'ah* are quite comprehensive and far-reaching. They are also rather complex, amongst the most complicated in all of the Talmud. There are various kinds of impurity, brought on by a number of different circumstances. No matter what occasions them, or for how long a period they last, they have the effect of prohibiting the person so "contaminated" from eating any sacred object, such as sacrificial meat or the priestly tithe, or from entering the sacred precincts of the Temple. Each form of *tum'ah* has a specifically prescribed procedure to revoke it and allow the defiled individual to regain the state of *taharah* or purity. However, there is one element that is common to all forms of *taharah*, and that is immersion in a *mikvah*, which is the climax of every procedure of purification.

What, in the larger sense, is it that under-lies all forms of *tum'ah*, and in what way, in the same sense, does *mikvah* neutralize the principle of *tum'ah*?

A *Whisper of Death*

The answer goes to the very core of Judaism and its orientation towards human life and values, and, incidentally, it provides new and fresh insights into the institution of Family Purity.

The Torah is a "Torah of Life." Judaism taught the principle of "reverence for life" long before it was preached by Albert Schweitzer. "It is a *tree of life* for them that lay hold of it" (Proverbs 3: 18). This was said in reference to Torah. The Torah itself defines for us the purpose of all the commandments: "and he shall live by them"—"and not die" (Lev. 18: 5; *Sanhedrin* 74a).

Adam was permitted to eat vegetables; he was forbidden to eat flesh. It was only later, in the days of Noah, that God, as a concession, allowed man to eat meat. This early vegetarianism is a powerful expression of Judaism's reverence for life. Whereas the priest in ancient Egypt, the land from which our people came out of a long exile, dedicated his life to death — he was a kind of religious undertaker — the priesthood in Israel was consecrated to life. The *Kohen* is forbidden to have any contact with death; with the exception of seven close relatives, he may not defile himself by coming under the same roof with a corpse.[1] To save a life it is permitted to transgress all commandments save three. Life is by all means one of the highest values of Torah Judaism.

---

[1] See commentary of Rabbi Samson Raphael Hirsch to Leviticus, beginning of Chap. XXI.

An analysis of the various species of *tum'ah* reveals that what they have in common is the awareness of death. The most potent source of impurity is, indeed, a corpse or a part thereof. The other kinds of *tum'ah* imply, indirectly, the suggestion of death, even if only the loss of potential life. For instance, the *metzora* (usually, though inaccurately, translated as leper) is in a state of *tum'ah*. This disease includes the withering or dying of the limbs of the leper (cf. Nu. 12: 12). That is why the Rabbis taught that a leper is considered as if he were dead. Hence, his leprosy puts him into a state of impurity. A man who suffers from "running issue" (possibly a form of gonorrhea) is impure. The issue is semen[2] and therefore the loss of potential life; or, if it is pus, it afflicts

<hr />

[2] See Tosefta *Zavim,* 2; cf. R. David Z. Hoffmann, *Sefer Va-yikra,* pp. 287f.

the organ of reproduction which is the source of life. Hence, the state of *tum'ah*. In the same manner, when a woman is *niddah*, during her menstruation, she loses an unfertilized ovum, and it is this loss of potential life, this whisper of death, that confers upon her the state of impurity. In childbirth, the mother has expelled from her body an organism that is or was alive,[3] and she is therefore considered impure.

Water: The Flame of Life

By the same token, *taharah* or purification is a reversal of the process of *tum'ah*. Just as *tum'ah* implies death, *taharah* implies life. And it is the *mikvah*, above all, that symbolizes the affirmation of life. For

---

[3] This answers the objection of Hoffmann, *ibid*. p. 217.

it is water that is the most potent symbol of life. "And the spirit of God hovered above the face of the water" (Gen. 1: 2). Fresh water is itself called, in Hebrew, *mayyim ḥayyim*, "living water." The Torah teaches that water covered the face of the entire earth and was the most abundant prominent substance in the world until God separated the waters (Gen. 1: 2, 6). The ancient Greek philosopher Thales consider-ed water the fundamental substance of the universe; although scientifically wrong, his insight is valuable.

Without water, life cannot be sustained. It is "indeed the matrix of life, not of ages past, but here and now..."[4] All organized living matter, from protoplasm through man, is in itself essentially watery. The average

---

[4] Sylvia Scapa, "What is Water?", *Main Currents in Modern Thought,* (January-February, 1965) p. 68.

early human embryo is 97% water, an adult man, 60%. Body water continues to diminish slowly with age, "as though the water content of the body were a measure of its vital activity. It would appear that the flame of life is sustained by water."[5]

When an astronomer today peers at some distant planet and wonders whether it sustains life, he first asks whether there is any water vapor in its atmosphere; if there is, life is a distinct possibility. Freudian psychologists recognize that in dreams and myths the ocean or water is a symbol of life, for man is born from a bag of water, the amniotic fluid of the mother. No wonder that in the *shemoneh esreh* prayer, when we praise God for His gift of rain, we include it in the second blessing, that which glorifies

---

[5] A. V. Wolf, "The Body of Water," *Scientific American* (November, 1958) p. 125.

God Who resurrects the dead. After drinking water we bless God "Who gives life to all the living." Water is, beyond all else, both a necessity and a symbol of life.

Similarly, when a non-Jew wishes to convert to Judaism and be received into the Covenant of Abraham, we require of him that he immerse himself in the *mikvah*. For the proselyte is considered a new individual, a new-born child, and the sense of birth, of new life, is emphasized by the *mikvah*. By emerging from the waters of the *mikvah*, a new Jew has been born to us.

So that *tum'ah*, the intimation of death, whether it be through *niddah* or any other form, is counteracted by immersion in the water of the *mikvah*, the symbol of life.

By means of this symbolism we may understand the special requirements for a *mikvah*. The *mikvah* must be a gathering of *natural* water, such as a well or lake or rainwater, and not a pool or bath, artificially accumulated by such means as plumbing. The question "what is the difference between (natural) water and (artificial) water?" already perplexed the ancients.[6] According to what has been said above concerning the symbolic significance of water, we may begin to appreciate the difference between the two. By insisting upon the naturalness of the waters of the *mikvah*, we affirm that God alone is the Author of Life, and to

---

[6] Interestingly, there *is* a difference between them despite the fact that they are chemically identical. Giogio Piccardi, professor of physical chemistry at Genoa University, in his *The Chemical Basis of Medical Climatology* (Springfield, Ill., 1962) Chap. II, writes of biological properties of water that are apparently unconnected with chemical composition: "Why is it that natural water drunk at a spring is more effective from a medical point of view than the same water bottled and aged. . . in spite of the fact that the difference in chemical composition reveals nothing in particular?"

Him and Him alone do we turn for con-
tinued life for us and our descendants after
us. Man is not the absolute master of his
life and destiny; *mayyim she'uvim*, water
artificially accumulated, does not therefore
possess the power of purification that apper-
tains to natural water. Life is of God.

An Education in Life

There is hardly a more important theme
in the world of today than the sanctity of
life. Life is, indeed, in eclipse. Its duration
may be longer, but its vulnerability to mass
destruction has never been more pro-
nounced. We are told to "enjoy life," yet
the sense of fulfillment and happiness is
rare. Life has been denied meaning — how
can anything described as "a biochemical
accident" be meaningful? — and consequently cheapened. Our contemporary gen-

eration has grown up conditioned to the possibility of sudden, total oblivion as a "natural" part of its existence. Conceived under a mushroom cloud, born into a world of nuclear hostility, weaned on radioactive strontium, it accepts with graceful callousness such ideas as "overkill" and nuclear proliferation. Life threatens to lose its distinctiveness, its value, its preciousness.

Unless we make a conscious effort to create an environment of radically different values, this is the poison our children will inhale: contempt for life and indifference to death. If we keep silent and allow "Nature" to "take its course," we condemn our sons and daughters to totter unsupported on the brink of nuclear holocaust. What can *anything* mean to people whose gaze is ever fixed into the gaping black hole of atomic destruction? Why love, why honor, why hope, if one must always be ready for mass extermination? Why parents, why home, why children, if tomorrow all may be reduced to a uniform radioactive ash?

A Jewish home, lived according to the noble code of the Jewish "way," is a nursery of life's sanctity. The love of life, and an inner appreciation of its unutterable sublimity, is an integral part of a Jewish environment. A child learns — not by mere words, but by experience and example — that Jews do not hunt; that their abhorrence of blood-lust extends even to salting meat in order to remove the blood; that one must extend his kindness to all creatures; that the enhancement of life is one of the chief concerns of the Torah.

Such a life-affirming milieu, which can do so very much towards imbuing a child with respect for the meaningfulness of life, must be created by parents. And they must be *committed* parents — parents who will carry out in the details of practice the high ideals of Judaism concerning the preciousness of life; parents who will be willing to commit their "way" in life to the life-"way" of Judaism.

Family Purity represents, as we have attempted to show, the joyous Jewish affirmation of life and the abhorrence of death and suffering. The institution of the *mikvah*, through the symbol of the waters, offers the possibility of a magnificent beginning for human life in love with life.

The time to start is not tomorrow. It is today. We owe it to children whom we bring into a world in which life is in such jeopardy, to give them, along with physical existence, the spiritual vitality symbolized and engendered by *taharat ha-mishpahah*, along with all the other precepts of Judaism.

This Jewish affirmation of life is a process of education. But it is too important to start when a child reaches school age. It must begin even before the child is conceived. Family Purity is that life-long education in the love of life which commences even before life begins.

VI.

In Practice

In Chapter II we referred to a number of booklets detailing the laws of Family Purity. Here we offer a brief description of these laws, in summary fashion.

Before the Wedding

When the date of the wedding approaches, the bride prepares herself in the following way. After making sure that her last period has completely ended, she counts seven consecutive days free from any menstrual discharge. After these seven days, she visits the *mikvah* in order to carry out the religious act of immersion (*tevillah*). She may do this during the day or in the evening.

In preparation for the immersion, the bride washes and combs her hair, removes nail varnish, trims her nails, removes rings, plaster, etc., and takes a bath.

Then, in the presence of the lady attendant (who is available with advice and assistance whenever needed), she immerses herself completely in the *mikvah*, and then says the following benediction:

"Blessed art Thou, O Lord our God, King of the universe, who has sanctified us by His commandments and commanded us concerning *tevillah*."

A beautiful, moving prayer has been composed for the bride to recite on this occasion. It has been included, in English translation, in the next chapter.

The Newly Wed

After the consumption of the marriage, the newlywed partners separate. Separate beds are essential during the ensuing days, just as for the period after menstruation. (This is an important point to bear in mind when buying the furniture for the new home.)

As explained above, all physical contact between the two partners is avoided during the period of separation. The wisdom of this is obvious, for the slightest touch or contact can arouse sexual feelings, and during these times husband and wife act towards each other with respect and affection but without any physical expression of love.

This period of separation lasts eleven days, the last seven of which should reveal complete freedom from any discharge. On the eleventh day, the necessary cleansing routine is carried out in preparation for immersion. After immersion in the *mikvah* (which must take place after nightfall), the marital relationships may be resumed.

Married Life

From then on throughout the marriage, the partners separate the night before the period is due. If menstruation does not ensue as anticipated, and one has ascertained this carefully, marital relations may be resumed.

From the commencement of menstruation, the wife counts a minimum of five days, during which all menstrual flow should normally have come to an end. Once it has been established without a doubt that all discharge has ceased, a bath is taken and there should be a change of underwear and bed linen. Seven further days are then counted, each of which must be completely free from discharge, and on the seventh day, the necessary preparatory cleansing should be carried out as described above. The immersion then takes place in the *mikvah* after nightfall.

And so husband and wife re-unite each month, their love refreshed, after the period of separation, finding each other once again in purity and love as they did on their wedding night.

Motherhood

After childbirth, as in the usual periods of separation, husband and wife have no physical contact until after the wife's visit to the *mikvah*. A minimum of seven days for a boy, and fourteen for a girl, should be allowed after childbirth; if the discharge has ceased by that time, a further seven clean days should be allowed for a recovery period. The usual preparatory cleansing is carried out, followed by immersion in the *mikvah*.

It is customary for the mother to visit the Synagogue and offer her thanksgiving to the Almighty for her recovery from childbirth, with an ardent prayer for the future well-being of the new-born baby. It is in fact the custom that this visit to the Synagogue is the first undertaken outside the house after the birth of the baby. This is how Jewish mothers show that their gratitude to God takes precedence over all their personal interests.

VII.

A Bride's Prayer*

May it be Thy will that Thy presence
dwell between my husband and me, and
that Thou unify Thy Holy Name through
us. Introduce into our hearts the spirit
of sanctity, and remove from us all evil
thoughts and plans. Give to my husband
and to me purity of soul, that neither of
us fix our gaze upon any other person in
the world, but that I should regard only
him, and he, only me. May he be in my eyes

---

*Translated and abbreviated from a prayer recorded
in *Hupat Hatanim* by Rabbi Raphael Meldola
(1754-1828) of Venice, to be recited before the
immersion.

as if there were no other man in the world as good, as handsome, and as charming; and may I be in the eyes of my husband as if there were no other woman in the world as beautiful, as charming, and as fitting for him. May his thought always be about me, and about no one else, as it is written, "Therefore shall a man leave his father and his mother and cleave to his wife."

And may it be Thy will, O Lord God, that our marriage prosper; that it be a marriage that will accord with the laws of Moses and Judaism; a marriage endowed with reverence for God and the fear of sin; a marriage in which will be realized the verse, "Your wife shall be like a fruitful vine in the interior of your house, your children like olive plants around your table"; a marriage wherein my husband will rejoice in me more than in all the delights of the world, as it is written, "A house and wealth is the inheritance of fathers, but only from the Lord is a wise wife"; a marriage in which there will never come between my husband and me any anger or bitterness, any jealousy or envy, but in which there will be between us only love and fraternity and peace and comradeship, humility and meekness and patience; a marriage in which there will be practiced love and charity and kindliness, and the doing of good deeds to all creatures; a marriage which will yield children who will endure, who will be decent, righteous, wholesome, and honorable, who will be healthy and good, in whom there will be no flaw, no defect, no illness, no disease, no injury, no pain, no weakness, no failure, and who will not lack good all the days of their life; a marriage wherein Thou wilt bestow upon our souls and our bodies holiness and purity in thought, speech, and action as befits good Jews; a marriage of prosperity and blessing, blessings of Heaven above and blessings of the deep couching below, blessings of health and fertility.

Now therefore, in order to unite Thy Holy Name in fear and in love, I prepare for this immersion according to the laws of Moses and Israel. May it be Thy will, O Lord God, that Thou purify us and sanctify us with Thy holiness; that Thou find us and our deeds acceptable, and give us the privilege of doing Thy will at all times, all the days of our life; and bless us with Thy blessings, for Thou art the Source of all blessings forever.

Blessed be the Lord forever, Amen.

VIII.

A Concluding Note

A number of ideas have here been presented to explain meaningfully a sacred institution which is crucial both to the perpetuation of Judaism and the Jewish people, and to the stability and happiness of the individual Jewish family.

In no way should it be imagined that this is the last word on a theme that is as old as the people of Israel, as sacred as the Sabbath or Yom Kippur or the Dietary Laws, and that entails such exalted ideals as the sanctity of time and of life itself.

If the reader has found some merit in the laws of *taharath ha-mishpaḥah* as here discussed, he should not let the matter rest merely with general assent or the expression of mild interest. The future of one's marriage and the perpetuation of Judaism are too important for half-hearted reactions. The cumulative experience of the Jewish people has confirmed the wise principle that no religious precept is meaningful unless faithfully practiced.

It is the hope and the prayer — and the plea — of the author that the reader be inspired to read further and, above all, to practice fully and faithfully the precept of Family Purity; to encourage other individuals to do so; and to support the Jewish community at large in making the proper facilities available for such observance.

"R. Akiva said: Happy are you, O Israel! Before whom do you purify yourselves? And who purifies you? — your Father in Heaven

... even as the *mikvah* purifies the impure, so does the Holy One purify Israel."

— Mishnah, *Yoma,* 8: 9

THE ROYAL REACH

*Discourses on the Jewish Tradition
and the World Today*

Rabbi Norman Lamm, one of the most eloquent expositors of modern Orthodox Judaism, offers insights from the Jewish tradition on a wide array of subjects from the Quest for the Supernatural to the Ethics of Protest, the conquest of the moon to the problems of the Six Day War, Jewish Mothers to the Pursuit of Fun.

The author notes a series of challenges posed to Judaism, both from the current crises that afflict our world and from within the inner life of Judaism itself. He describes the reactions of Judaism as themselves constituting a challenge to achieve what he calls The Royal Reach — "a majestic craving for high goals and sublime ends far beyond the petty ambitions" that pre-occupy most of our waking hours. Judaism induces in its adherents "a turbulence of the spirit . . . a quivering of the soul as it inches to the border of self-doubt and leaps over it into self-transcendence, and a convulsive self-transformation of human striving and definition of ends."

cloth   356 pages   **$11.95**

FELDHEIM PUBLISHERS - JERUSALEM/NEWYORK